Sammy Sunshine   Arthur   Ted   Ron

Bill   Terry

Coat of arms of the Rowe family

MY
BROTHERS
IN ARMS

7 WENT TO WAR

6 CAME HOME

This is the story of seven brothers
who joined up in the armed services
to see action in the Second World
War.

~

Brother 1 - Phillip in the Army with the Desert Rats
D Day

~

Brother 2 - Alf in the RAF in Algiers Africa

~

Brother 3 - Arthur Fleet Air Arm in India

~

Brother 4 –Ted 15year old Boy Seaman on Russian Convoys

~

Brother 5 - Bill Boy Seaman in Navy Atlantic convoys and D Day Landings

~

Brother 6 – Ron Boy Seaman in the Navy in the Far-East

~

Brother 7 - Tom Royal Canadian Engineers in the D Day Landings (While unbeknownst to him, his younger brother Bill was on ship HMS Ramillies covering them with its heavy guns on his 16th Birthday.

<u>TOM WAS SHOT THE DAY AFTER V-E DAY</u>

Table of Contents

PHILLIP

Brother No.1 Phillip

Oldest brother Phillip was the first brother to go to war in 1938. He was in the Household Cavalry guarding the Queen on their wonderful horses outside Buckingham Palace. They were sent off to the Middle East with their horses to guard the oil pipelines from saboteurs in the desert.

My younger brother was just five years old, and I just seven, when we waved him goodbye as he climbed up the stairs of the local bus with his putties around his legs, disappearing up the stairs on his way to Bournemouth station, back to his barracks in London. This was 1937.

I didn't see him again for more than twenty years. This was because at the age of eleven we younger boys in our family of ten children were sent off to a naval orphanage as Dad was widowed and left with his family of ten, all under the age of seventeen. Then we were put into the Royal Navy and made to sign up for fourteen years. Six of us boys ended up in the Navy at sea.

So with my four years in the orphanage it was my turn to join the Royal Navy in 1946. I always say that in 1946 I waited to see who was winning the war. This is the reason I lost track of my brother Phillip for fifteen long years as we were all away from home in some sort of uniform or other. It wasn't until twenty-three years later, after serving my fourteen years in the Royal Navy, getting married with two children, that I was able to drive up to London and introduce him to my lovely wife and two children.

His regiment disbanded their horses when the war broke out in the desert and they were switched over to a three man high tank regiment as part of the Eighth Army against Rommel. He was a clever artist and used to send his drawings home to father during the desert campaign. He took part in the Salerno landings, then the regiment fought right up through Italy into Germany, until the end. He was fighting for 7 years, from 1938 till 1945 !

I was at sea and missed his homecoming. Dad was still a serving policeman. Brother Phillip came home on leave and was pleased to sleep in a proper bed, back home, but waking up in the night for a cigarette he would rub his cigarette butt out on the bedroom wallpaper above his head. Father lost his temper and kicked him out of the house! He evidently finished his leave with his girlfriend.

After his leave and back with his regiment in the horse barracks. He couldn't wait for his demob. He deserted from the Cavalry and as we learnt he was staying with one of his other girlfriends nearby. However, father P.C. Rowe was checking in at his 9am police muster, taking notes for the day from the sergeant, when there was an alert for a soldier who had deserted from the Army. As the deserter's description was read out, his father, P.C. Rowe, suddenly recognised that he knew the deserter very well. It was his son!

One of my other older brothers, home on leave from the Navy, went round and told our uncle, who came to the rescue, and convinced Brother Phillip to return to his barracks. He did and was put on jankers. I heard these stories when I was next home on leave.

I started to correspond with him when I got out of the Navy. My wife and I drove up to visit him when he was in hospital around 1970. When we got to the hospital at his bedside the nurse warned us that he was heavily dosed on drugs and was a little incoherent. We started chatting. When I told him that I had been unwell with chronic constipation, he replied that he was constipated in the desert in 1944. With that I leaned over to open the window and said '1944 Crikey, we'd better open all the windows!' with that the nurses fell about laughing.

We never met his dear wife as she had died earlier. We had heard stories that he was a clairvoyant and would get premonitions of unnatural events. The Daily Mirror of the day in 1960 used to print off various predictions; they printed one of brother Phillip's predictions, that there would be a Royal shooting involving a car. Later on, it happened with Princess Anne's car being threatened.

A second prediction he sent them was that a school would be damaged with a landslide and children would be injured. Later on, we had the terrible Aberfan coal slide disaster. Before this book goes to print, I will try and get the copies of the predictions from the newspaper. When the Aberfan disaster happened, I was entertaining nearby with a trio clown act called 'The Super Sausage Squad' at a miners' gala. We heard that the local Assembly Hall was being used as a rehab rescue centre, so the three of us dressed back up in our clown regalia and stayed over.

No. 1 Me as Sailor Sam

No. 2 Kerby Drill (The road safety clown now sadly passed away at 97 years old)

No. 3 Captain Jim (Kerby's son)

We stayed the night and drove home the next day. When my late wife put my clown clothes through the washing machine, she wanted to know what all the black dust was in the bottom of the machine. Such a terrible tragedy.

Phillip re-married, and the next time I saw him he was in hospital, very poorly, and never got over his problem from which he passed away.

ALF

Brother No.2 – Alf

My next eldest brother to go away to war was brother Alf. He started as a carpenter and joiner, apprenticed at the age of fourteen, as they did in the 30's. A lifelong story about him, handed down through the family, haunted me through the years. Being sent away to a naval orphanage in 1942, then into the Navy as a fifteen-year-old boy, I lost contact of events so wasn't sure how true some of these family stories were, or how exaggerated or altered.

However, the story was that one day when brother Alf came home from working at his apprenticeship at just sixteen years old, he heard screaming in the kitchen of our Police house. When he got in he confronted my father belting his younger brother Arthur, who was just fourteen years old. He pleaded for father to stop, but father carried on. At that point sixteen-year-old Alf took the bread knife out of the drawer and chased Dad up the road, holding his trousers up as he'd left his belt on the kitchen floor! Well, this story stuck with me for over eighty years as the most memorable one.

However, eighty years on in 2016 both of us, Brother Alf and I had both lost our dear wives. Alf was very ill at his home and I managed to get there and stayed with him. In hospital we were reminiscing over old times and I asked him if it was true that he had chased our Dad up the street with a carving knife for whipping brother Arthur. He said Sam, it's nearly true, but it wasn't your brother he was whacking, it was our sister Connie, just sixteen years old, who was now housekeeper to our family of ten now that our mum had died.

I was able to stay with him until he passed away in 2016. When he turned eighteen and was called up into the RAF, he spent just a year in the famous Home Guard. My younger brother Terry and I, who were the youngest of ten in the family, just nine and seven years old, thought it was great fun watching our brother Alf doing marching drill and bayonet charges with a broom handle into sandbags hanging from the goal post out on Redhill Common.

Things changed dramatically when real rifles turned up and Brother Alf brought a real Bren gun indoors on his way to guard Hurn Airport one night. In the woods nearby they used to do manoeuvres and hide to ambush the enemy to stop them from getting through. Us kids would shout and tell them where they were hiding! One weekend things went horribly wrong when there was an accident with a hand grenade.

It eventually came time for Alf to be called up, He was enlisted into the RAF Police and away went brother No.2 off to war. He was posted abroad. I never saw him go as I had just been put on a train at Bournemouth and sent off up to a naval school on the east coast at just aged eleven. He ended up stationed in North Africa near Algeria. Unbeknownst to him, one of his younger brothers, Brother No.5 Bill, had been sent to sea as a fifteen-year-old Boy Seaman. He was on Atlantic convoy escort duties aboard the battleship H.M.S. Ramillies, whose 16" guns are on display outside the Imperial War Museum in London.

Well, at this early time during the war, sailor Bill found him and his shipmates anchored off the Port of Algiers. So he went ashore with the view of a good run ashore with a couple of his messmates to sample the watering holes. Meeting up with a couple of R.A.F. Police in a bar, he mentioned that his brother Alf, who was then a Corporal in the R.A.F. Police, was stationed near Algiers. They said 'jump in the jeep and we'll take you to his camp'.

There he was asleep on his camp bed in the desert where the two "Jolly Jacks" tipped him out of his bunk saying 'come on brother, wakey wakey, get your gear on and show us what we're missing in the bright lights of Algiers.' You couldn't have arranged that! Well Bill, Brother No.5, went sailing off the next day with double vision and a hangover, so we'll meet Bill in the mid-Atlantic later on.

Back to Alf, Brother No.2, policing in the Algerian desert. After a while he had a pleasant posting back to the UK for a crash course to pick up guard dogs to take back to the RAF storage depots in the Algerian desert, where they were having problems with the locals breaking into the stores and stealing from them. It was known for a lorry to drive through a busy Arab town and getting through back out the other end of the village where the RAF driver would find that the spare wheel had been stolen off the back of his truck.

They were sent back to the UK to be trained with new guard dogs for them to take back to their depots in the desert to scare off the thieves from breaking in and stealing the goods. Many years later after the war, when we occasionally met up, I remember Brother Alf telling me that the dogs helped to solve part of the problem, but when the thieves started stripping off their clothes and covering their bodies in grease and wild animal fat to scare the dogs off, they had a problem.

Alf was promoted up to Sergeant and at one time was considering making a career of it. However a particular series of events soured his ambitions and entirely turned him against the Service for a career.

He had to spend the last 24 hours guarding a deserter who was being executed by firing squad in the morning. Duty had to be done, but he told me that he couldn't get the experience out of his mind. He decided that justice had to be done to help him make this decision to get back to normality, or it may have been the fact that he met a very nice WAAF service lady that joined their squadron towards the end of the campaign. With both getting demobbed they were soon married and settled down to raise a family.

ARTHUR

Brother No.3 – Arthur

The next Brother to go to war was Brother No.3, Arthur, the plumber, just 2 years, he'd served in the Home Guard playing soldiers. When he came of the age of eighteen, they didn't call him up as his skill was used at Hurn Airport for pipe laying and installations. This was short-lived when he got his call up papers and he joined the Fleet Air Arm. So up to now three of the Rowe boys were in uniform. One in each of the three Services.

Before we follow Brother No.3 I must pause to tell you a bit more about the development of Hurn Airport near Bournemouth. It soon became very active and was sealed off to the public. However my younger brother Terry and I would trek out there through the bushes off the beaten track, and get right up to the perimeter fence, peeping through. Amongst the gliders the Black American Soldiers were sorting their equipment out.

They had a huge sand wheel where they were sharpening their knives and bayonets, to us kids just seven and nine years old it was so exciting. If our Dad had found out, it would be Samuel in the front room and whack! Some 70 years on from this I was performing at an Esso garage opening when I got talking to an old boy who was sweeping up on the forecourt. On finding out I lived near Bournemouth he said that he was stationed at Bournemouth Airport during the war, in the Parachute Regiment. I repeated to him about what us kids had seen, he said that his lads carried and concealed four commandos' knives on their person. One down each leg and two up high on their shoulders, so if they had to put their hand up on their heads, they still had swift access to the two weapons!

Back to 1940 and Brother No.3 Arthur the plumber, who had just been called up into active service, was cycling home from pipe laying preparing the airport runways. He came home up our road, Redhill Drive, when my nipper brother called me out of the gate. Big brother's plumber's bicycle had snapped in half coming up the hill with the weight of all his extra tools. We ran to meet him and helped him with half the bike frame each. He wasn't going to need them where he was going up to the Naval Fleet Air Arm…

I missed him tremendously when he left home to join up. We'd lost our Mum two years earlier, our sister Connie was now our Mum, at the age of sixteen she had been housekeeping since leaving school at fourteen when mum passed away. She kept the whole house clean and cooked all our meals, Dad's dinner had to be ready when he arrived home on his Police bike. Brother Arthur was so good to us two younger boys and sister Beryl.

We were home after the older ones were serving, and Ron was up in the Naval Orphanage at the age of eleven where we were due to go up on the East Coast as we reached eleven years old. Brother Arthur built toys like bows and arrows, and an old pram go-cart that was great fun. Our pocket money of one penny a week each Saturday didn't go far, but Arthur bought us sweets, as Dad forbade him to give us pocket money.

On Sundays father gave us another penny to put into the collection at the Church where he sent all three of us, Terry, me and sister Beryl, every Sunday. However on the way to Church in Moordown, Bournemouth, we found a small tuck shop where we could buy a bag of sweets for half a penny. Great, as it meant sweeties for us and we still had half a penny change for him up there! All went well for ages until one dull Sunday morning as we came out of the tuck shop, who was standing at the end of the turning but P.C. Father Rowe, sitting on his Police bicycle, telling me to spit out the sweets and take the bag back to the shop ... and I'll see you after I get off duty, now get to Church. Well I never really prayed before, and it didn't help much, (he'd got home before we got home). After pleading to Jesus for forgiveness, no dinner that day, and a good whacking in the front room!

Now it was my turn as I reached eleven to be put on the train at Bournemouth up to the East Coast to join the Naval orphanage. We were allowed home for two weeks at Christmas when luckily enough Arthur managed to get home for a break. On telling him that the dormitory that we slept in was blacked out for the air raids coming over, and though the dormitories were huge, with over forty lads in, my bunk head was against the only radio speaker, but they switched it off at 8pm.

However Brother Arthur said he had something in his kit bag that I could have. It was a set of earphones that I could plug into the back of the speaker and no one else would hear. I could be in my own little world! Well I couldn't wait to try them out, it made the burden of going back to the snake pit a little less rotten.

Sure enough, they worked a treat. During the day I rolled them up in my long socks away from spot checks meant to find any hidden apples that used to be nicked and put in our cupboards, although we called it scrumping from the nearby farm out of bounds. I became a celebrity overnight. They couldn't work out how I knew about the D Day landings the very next day! I was never found out the whole time. I spun a yarn that I dreamt a lot!

Arthur sailed off to India to set up a small runway for the Fleet Air Arm squadron. Many years later the tales he told of setting up the huts near the jungle. They had some resident Army engineers already there to welcome them, "Right" the sergeant said "the area is known for its snakes. Each morning shake out your boots in case one has settled in overnight". Evidently in the middle of one night a scream came from the bucket loo outside, a lad came running in, showing his bare bum screaming that a snake had bitten his backside. Sure enough they could see the two marks on his skin. "Well" one lad said, "now will find out who your real friend who has to suck the poison out" Suddenly a rifle goes off outside, a guy comes in holding up the culprit, a dead chicken that was sat in the loo.

Brother Arthur was happy being ashore at the air strip and was only too pleased to finish his service back in the UK, working on <u>Target A/c</u> until he was demobbed.

TED

Brother No.4 – Ted

Now Brother No.4 was Brother Ted, who was the first eleven-year-old son of the family to be sent to the Naval orphanage up on the East coast, in 1931, with four more of his younger brothers following every two years. Doing four years there, then being put in the Navy for twelve years, being made to sign on at the age of just fifteen. Hence three of them ended up spending their sixteenth birthday at sea during the war. This Brother Ted at fifteen spent his sixteenth birthday on board a small corvette escorting the Russian convoys. He has told me that they were on the upper deck chipping ice off the rigging so they wouldn't capsize. On the third week they arrived in the Russian Port, put their gangway down and the Russians put a sentry on duty controlling their exit ashore. So after dark, they inflated their rubber dinghies and paddled further along the jetty to get to the vodka!

The Russian Government awarded all those that served on the Russian convoys with a medal, but the British Government had forbidden them to wear it. Guess what, over sixty years later, the British Government struck its own version of the Russian convoy crews medal and sent them out to those who were still alive, although a lot of them were sent back in disgust.

Ted got injured when his gun got blown up in the Far East and came home on HMS Vanguard in 1946. HMS Vanguard brought the Princess home from South Africa into Portsmouth harbour in 1946. Coincidently, as I have mentioned earlier, that was the year that I was put into the Navy. However, due to public pressure for fifteen year olds not to be enrolled any more, The Admiralty later issued an order giving us the choice to resign after only seven years instead of fifteen years, then demob and spend five years on reserve. I just scraped in as so many resigned. <u>The Admiralty cancelled it but I managed to let my younger brother Terry who was stationed up in Scotland know so all thirty of his Boy Seaman managed to get their freedom back early.</u>

However, back to HMS Vanguard now alongside Portsmouth. Well, I was six months in the Navy, stationed across the harbour in HMS St Vincent, Gosport, and Brother Ted managed to contact me.

Meanwhile all the Boy Seamen at HMS Vincent, all four hundred of us, were marched into Portsmouth docks to line the route through the dockyard for the Royal cars carrying all the Royalty to come past. They talked about the Queen's reign, well that day was my first start of a long experience of the Queen's rain we got soaking wet. Many years later I was still standing in the rain waiting for various Royalties. We had no spin driers in those days, and no washing machines. It was all hand-drolic!

However, Brother Ted invited me aboard HMS Vanguard one Sunday when I was off duty, and he promised to save some of his tot of rum if I could make it. Well I had some money left over from my 2/6^d a week for the ferry. I crossed Pompey harbour on the ferry and climbed up the gangway of HMS Vanguard, the largest battleship left in the fleet. It never fired a gun in anger as it was not ready until after the war. I got below decks looking for my Brother's mess and found him just in time; he had saved me his tot of rum. Sixteen-year-old boy seaman, Up Spirits! Stand fast the Holy Ghost! My first tot of rum.

However two years later at eighteen I was entitled to my first tot. In the lower deck your tot is watered down, one tot measure of rum with a similar measure of water, hence it's called a two in one tot. This is so that the lower deck wouldn't bottle it, saving up the neat rum, get drunk, and start a fight. The traditional rum issued was a gift from the Caribbean Isle as a thank you for cleaning their harbours of pirates. However come 1973, with nuclear weapons on board ship, the Admiralty thought it wise to cancel the daily rum issue in case of an accident on the nuclear button.

However Ted was admitted into Hasla Hospital for treatment and check over his previous injuries when he got blown up at sea. He got released out of the service and married to a local girl near my parents' home, so I saw him when I was able to get home on leave. This was difficult on just 2/6^{d} a week.

BILL

Brother No.5 – Bill

Brother No.5 was Brother Bill. He was put into the Navy in 1941. His first ship was the battleship Ramillies on convoy duties in the Atlantic, as I've mentioned earlier. Part of their duties during the night-time was as lookout for U Boats from the bridge, posting four hours at a time. This particular night Bill had the middle watch, midnight till four am. Before you go out in the pitch dark you have to spend fifteen minutes in a darkened booth, lit only with a red light, to get your eyes right so that you can see straight away in the pitch dark.

Also to keep warm, you were allowed to wear as much warm clothing as you liked, providing it was covered by the standard duffel coat that crew and officers wore on watch. Well brother Bill knew that he was relieving his mess mate Soapy Watson. So he crept up behind him, put his hand up the back of his duffel coat and said 'OK Soapy, I got the weight' but it wasn't his mate soapy it was the Captain of the Ship!

'Good God what on Earth!' Bill letting go of the skipper's coat while saluting with both hands, 'Sorry Sir, Sorry Sir' ....'You will be lad if this gets any further from here'. Soapy had been sent off to fetch something for the Captain, below Brother Bill was promoted Grabber 1st Class.

His ship's next operation was bombarding with their 16" heavy guns at the Normandy D Day landings, knocking out the German Heavy shore guns. The spotters cleared them to move in closer, when here was a huge whistle overhead, and a German salvo splashed astern of them. Panic! 'Full astern' shouted the skipper. The Jerrys had hidden guns on railway tracks in the cliffs. Bill spent his sixteenth birthday as a Boy Seaman during those landings. He said that they never undressed for three days. His Brother Tom was landing on the beach at the same time.

On the 60th Anniversary of D Day I took Brother Bill to the British Legion 60th Anniversary back over to Normandy. Part of the ceremony was an invitation by the French Mayor of Caen at his Civil Hall, where all the veterans were presented with a large medal plaque. As their names were called out they stepped forward and a French school child presented it to each Serviceman. I had a lump in my throat. 'This is for all your Brothers I said'. When they called Brother Bill up, the school child was a six-foot student and Bill said 'I ain't gonna kiss you mate'. The French people made us very welcome throughout the three-day trip.

People often ask with five of us Brothers serving in the Navy, did we ever serve on the same ship together? Well it was in peacetime about 1954 that after living on a destroyer for five years I got drafted to carrier HMS Vengeance, only to find that my Brother Bill was on board. He was a Seaman torpedo man, or electrician as known today. I was a Leading Seaman diver by then. What a different lifestyle playing deck hockey on the flight deck, films shown in the aircraft hangar. Our own concert parties on the aircraft lift with scene changes going on back up to the flight deck. We had a good run ashore together in Oslo, Norway, where we picked up a lovely stray St Bernard dog which we smuggled on board as we disappeared into our hammocks. The dog gate-crashed the Officers cocktail party on the quarter deck and cocked his leg over the ornamental dolphins, before being escorted ashore by a Royal Marine escort.

The biggest favour that Brother Bill did for his two younger brothers, me and Terry, was to tell us due to the public questioning why Boys of fifteen from the Naval orphanage were made to sign on for fourteen years in the Navy. The poor boys from sixteen onwards, were being lost at sea. For example the boys on HMS Hood were not killed immediately, that German salvo split her in half, and the majority of the boys and crew were buried alive when the ship hurtled to the bottom of the dark ocean, trapped in their various small compartments to either slowly drown as the water crept around them, or slowly run out of oxygen. That's why the Navy is called 'The Senior Service!', Because of the outcry my Brother Bill said it's too late for me, but the Admiralty have just brought out a new Admiralty Fleet Order that any serving boy ratings that joined before July 1946 and had been made to sign for fourteen years, can resign for seven then be demobbed with five years on reserve. Well I have already told you how me and my younger brother Terry went for it and owed Bill our freedom.

We were at sea one night when I got a message that my Brother Bill was in trouble down in his mess deck. My mate and I nipped down to find Bill had swung up into his Hammock which had split right down the middle and there he was flat out on the iron deck, not being able to move. He got up OK after the medic OK'd him.

Bill was the smart boy amongst all the Rowe Boys. I'd learnt to cut hair when I was sick on light duty as a Boy Seaman, after being dropped twenty feet on my back doing life boat drill. I could earn extra pocket money on board ship cutting hair. One Saturday when we were alongside visiting Oslo, Brother Bill bugged me to go for a run ashore and have a beer or two. 'Sorry Bill I'm broke', 'we'll set up your hair cutting in the canteen flat for a while and we'll go ashore this evening. My mate who is a Chief Petty Officer on duty on the gangway. As the lads go ashore he'll turn some down to you to get their scruffy haircut. After about half an hour I had to bring him back to say 'No more, there's enough here, see you on the jetty'.

It was 1950 when I got drafted to a smaller ship a destroyer up in Scotland when I got a parcel posted to me. Well that was a first in nine years. It was a pile of raffle tickets, as Brother Bill was holding an Easter raffle to raffle his Austin Seven car back in Pompey, where he used it to get home to his newly-wedded wife, and sometimes we'd get a lift home to Ringwood for the weekend. He wanted me to sell the tickets to the lads on the Pompey ships that would be back down in NAFFI club in Pompey over the Easter break.

It was a great success, all tickets sold. One lucky matelot won his car! Meeting Bill at the bar I said 'we'll have to get the train home now'. 'No Sam, he said, we're going in the Austin Seven, 'But it's gone'. 'No it hasn't' he said, 'it's round the back and this is my last pint I'll see you round there. 'Oh no' I said' 'I'm not riding out of Pompey in the Austin, I'll get the bus out to Cosham and wait for you at the bus stop'! Well Bill got married then got demobbed, They set up a paper shop in Wantage which they ran up to his retirement.

RON

Brother No.6 – Ron

Now Brother No.6 was Ron. He went to war and was posted to sail in a cruiser, out in the Far East. Then after the war he spent two and a half years posted in Hong Kong. When he came home after that commission his new baby daughter Janet was just two years old, and on seeing her Daddy for the first time she screamed the house down. After he had his month's leave at home, he returned to the Naval barracks in Portsmouth where he hoped to serve for a while, as he could get home every weekend to his new family as he lived just a half hour train ride away in Havant.

At that same time I was also stationed ashore at a Naval radar training base. Well at that time the Korean War broke out and I was drafted on the cruiser HMS Glasgow to sail out to Korea to assist the American Navy out there. I had been in the Navy six years by then without going abroad. My five brothers still serving in the Navy said 'It's about time you got some sea time Sam and got your knees brown'. I wasn't too thrilled about going out to the war zone. I had to pack my bag and hammock and take the train up to Chatham dockyard where I joined the cruiser HMS Glasgow. The same class cruiser as HMS Belfast alongside, berthed in the Thames in London today. The Glasgow was alongside being loaded with the necessary for war situations. Days and nights of handling provisions and ammo. The ship had just had a major refit which usually entails work up trials on compass setting, gunnery test etc. However they decided to steam down to Gibraltar and sort out any problems in the docks there. Things turned out in our favour as major problems cropped up with our main engines and couldn't be sorted out in time, so we sailed on into Malta dockyard.

When it was time to send a replacement cruiser out to the Korean campaign we were made flagship of the Mediterranean Fleet and became Lord Louis Mountbatten's flagship. A nice new lick of paint and we were ready to cruise the Med, however, another city class cruiser had to be re-commissioned to replace us and then off to the Korean coastal waters. A complete crew had to be found to man HMS Belfast.

Brother Ron had reported back to the Naval barracks, hoping for a cushy number, when he was drafted back on board a ship taking him and his shipmates back out to the Far East. I imagined that he wouldn't be too happy about his trip back out to the Far East. However we were soon to find out just how unhappy the lads who were replacing us were as we heard that their ship would be calling into Malta where we were starting to get a nice steady suntan.

Well the day her bows appeared at the entrance of the grand Harbour Malta and steamed slowly past us, the greetings were not very complimentary, especially when we could hear them singing 'Any old Iron, Any old iron', and we had just finished painting the ship and polishing the brass work.

Our lads were a bit too shy to go ashore and have a beer with them. Our Skipper made us go below decks as she passed us close on her way out to sea, but I did manage to get ashore and say 'Sorry bruv' over a few bottles of the local booze.

They had a few rough times out there patrolling the Korean Coast. The incident that hurt them most he told me when we got back to Pompey a couple of years later. They had to patrol at sea for a month, back in harbour when the American warship would come out to sea and relieve the British cruiser. Well they were back in alongside just three days after their spell at sea when they had an emergency to go back out. as their Yankee relief warship was unfit for sea and had to return back to harbour. The cause of the problem that made them unseaworthy was the fact that their entire ice water cooling system had broken down!

Out of the six of us Brothers who were put in the Naval orphanage, Ron was the only one who stayed in the Navy to make a career out of it.

TOMMY

Brother No.7 – Brother-in-law Tommy

Brother No.7 who went to War was Brother-in-law Captain Tommy, who married our dear sister Connie. He came into our family while he was drafted over with his regiment from Canada. He met Connie in the ice rink in Bournemouth. She was not allowed to go down there by my very strict father who was a policeman stationed in Bournemouth. But our dear sister Connie, as I mentioned earlier, came to our rescue when Mum passed away. My younger brother Terry was just four years old and I was nearly six. Then Connie was fourteen left school and became our Mother and housekeeper.

Now at the age of eighteen she became a very good ice skater but when war broke out and all the American and Canadian soldiers were passing the time waiting for D Day, they were out to make the best of their time in beautiful Bournemouth. Tommy met Connie in the Westover Ice Rink. The first time I met Tommy was when a car pulled up outside our gate one day and a very tall, very handsome soldier officer came over and asked if our sister Connie was at home. We said 'yes, and so is Father'. 'Oh great', he said, 'and would you show me in'. We nippers didn't know at the time but that's when he came and asked father PC Rowe for his daughter's hand in marriage!

Well, these very brave Canadians that came over to our rescue were just weeks away from putting their lives on the line. Within two weeks the wedding was on. My dear beautiful sister Connie was counting the days to go, getting everything ready. She was laying all her gear, our new suits and my sister Beryl's dress on top of our Anderson Shelter, which was a huge metal box frame with our double bed inside, where sister Beryl and her three younger brothers slept as a precaution against German bombers coming overlooking for Bournemouth Hurn Air Strip, which they never did find.

We sat and watched Connie curl her hair with the hair tongs that were heated in the fireplace in those days. We watched her shaving her eyebrows etc. getting ready for her big day. She went out early that evening with Tommy, Father and Step- Mother, but she had left her hair curlers on the fireplace, so

I had a go at curling my hair and shaving my eyebrows as a dare from my Brother! Hence in the wedding family photo there was me with curly hair and no eyebrows. Brother Tommy, as Captain Tommy of the Royal Canadian Engineers, the Colonel of his Regiment and fellow Officers all make a wonderful picture of a very special day.

Within weeks the time came for the D Day landings and Tommy and his fellow comrades went in under high bombardment, at the same time being covered with high16" shell bombardment from British battleship HMS Ramillies, whose huge 16" guns are as I said now on permanent display outside the British War Museum.

On board that ship, as the brave Canadians were fighting their way up the beaches, unbeknownst to him his new Brother-in-Law Bill, a sixteen-year-old boy Seaman, was loading ammo on board supporting them, as I mentioned earlier. In the meantime, Tommy's new wife sister Connie had joined the Women's Air Force, so was stationed away from home. During that time, I had been put in the Naval orphanage, hence the war came to a joyous end and everyone was celebrating.

VE Day. Connie was away stationed in the WAFS, when a few days after we got the news that our dear Brother Captain Tommy had been killed, shot the day after VE Day. Being away from home I didn't hear this for some time. Connie was never to see him again, she was evidently serving as a WAAF Officer at a station near Oxford, I was away at Naval school. We all felt it very bad. Captain Tommy's dear Mother, a widow and living on her own back in Canada, was no longer his next of kin. Sister Connie married again and moved to America. My dear late wife and I visited relatives in Canada some twenty years later and visited the Canadian House of Governors, where we found their Book of Remembrance, and with the help of the Sergeant At Arms, found our brother's Captain Tommy Greenhalgh's Page of Remembrance. When we got back home to the UK there was a large brown envelope with a Canadian Government stamp on the outside. Ashley, my son, thought his Dad had been arrested.

Whilst in Canada I was pleased to meet several Canadian ex-servicemen who had sailed over to help Britain in the war against Hitler. We in the UK will be forever grateful and will never forget the sacrifices that they made. The Canadians soldiers had a reputation of being very tough, efficient and excellent marksman making excellent commandos. All this is history now but must **NEVER BE FORGOTTEN**.

After the war years during the fifteen years in the Navy and Sammy losing contact with his family at home, he learnt of a very brave uncle called George Beeson, who joined the Army at seventeen years old. He was captured at Dunkirk while holding the Germans back to help the soldiers back to the UK. He was taken prisoner of War and forced to march for four days across Northern France and North Belgium. They were spat on, at night and were having their boots stolen when they were asleep. During his years as a POW he became WWII's most escaped prisoner as he escaped five times. The book about it was entitled "5 Roads to Freedom". The launching of the book stuttered a bit over some of their treatment on the march. On his final escape he stayed with the Free French fighters till their liberation. Many years later at his funeral near Brighton several ex Free French buddies of his came over to the UK to pay their respects.

At fifteen years old Sammy was home on leave from the Navy that he had been put into. He met another Uncle whom he never knew he had. This Uncle, named Harry Young, from Christchurch, had in 1938 arrived off the West coast of Ireland after sailing single-handed across the Atlantic from New York in a 15-foot-long sailing boat in 31 days, without a radio or navigation aids. He had built the boat himself. He got picked up by the Coast Guard and went to join the Royal Navy but failed on his eyesight. He joined the Merchant Navy and spent the War years sailing to and from the USA.

Sammy met him in 1946 for the first time at Christchurch river, where he showed him his boat that he was attempting to sail back across to the USA single-handed. He sailed around Great Britain and set sail from the West Coast of Ireland in August 1946. He was never to be seen again. The Villagers later said that they tried to stop him from leaving in terrible weather. His 1938 Atlantic crossing is mentioned in the sailing book titled "The

Big Book of Sailing" by Mr. Harry Young of
Christchurch, Hampshire. Published by Amazon.

PHOTOS

The cruiser HMS Glasgow

L/S. Sam Rowse

HM Queen Elizabeth II welcomed aboard HMS Glasgow 5/5/1954   (RP)

Queen Elizabeth and Prince Philip visiting
the HMS Glasgow in 1954

H.M.S. GLasgow, 10/4/1954

"Girl Guides Go Camping"   (SR)
AB Feltham   L/ Seaman Pinder   AB Wheatley   L/Seaman Rowe

5 grown sailors acting as Girl guides (I'm on the right!)

On board, we had our own comedy program to entertain the ship's crew.

("AB" means "able seaman", "L" means "leading seaman")

Sailor-Sam developed his humour after serving 11 years in Naval Service. Ending up as a diver in Suez Canal, after demob he became a Clown, a stilt-walker, a compere. He performed around the Globe!

Printed in Great Britain
by Amazon